CONTENTS

INTRODUCTION

 Self-hardening modelling clay is a modern development which has its roots in pottery. Although it cannot be worked by the traditional method on a wheel, it can be moulded, rolled, manipulated and cut just like real clay. This versatile medium has the qualities of its better-known counterpart, without the disadvantages. Real clay is messy and has to be fired before it can be finished, but self-hardening modelling clay can be cleared away quickly and left to dry in its own time. It has similarities too, to working with salt dough, since it does not require any specialist equipment or large working area set aside specifically for the task. Since this clay is available in white as well as traditional terracotta, colour can be added to the clay before it is shaped. Once dry, it can be decorated with anything from paint to gold leaf. No special glazes are required, just a couple of coats of varnish.

We have brought together 20 stunning projects for the home, ranging from a kitchen message board decorated with a three-dimensional hen, perfect for any country-style home, to opulent gilded tie-backs for lavish curtains and a textured lamp base with a quirky 1950s feel. Whether your style is to work on a large scale with a bright and cheerful colour scheme or for finely detailed, hand-crafted items in subtle tones, there is something here for everyone. If you feel daunted in any way, think back to the simple coil pots that you made as a child. How much fun it was, but also how simple! Have a go at the projects in this book and you will soon be hooked.

Deborah Barker

FLOWER GARDEN CHALK BOARD

Whether you want to jot down reminders for yourself or to leave important messages for somebody else, this little board in its pretty, rustic frame is perfect for the potting shed or to hang on the kitchen wall beside the back door.

YOU WILL NEED
wooden fruit crate
saw
mitre block (square)
wood glue
staple gun
acrylic paints in a variety of colours
small household and medium artist's paintbrushes
glue gun
small chalk board with old frame removed
modelling clay
modelling tools
greaseproof (waxed) paper
tracing paper
paper
pencil
scissors
rolling pin
sharp knife

1 To make the rustic frame, remove the sides of the fruit crate and from it cut four lengths to fit the board dimensions. Mitre the corners or join the ends together. Use wood glue, then a staple gun, to hold the joints firmly. Using a household paintbrush, paint the front of the new frame bright green. Allow to dry, then glue the chalk board behind the frame.

2 To model a flower, roll six balls of clay the same size. Put one ball aside until step 3. Squeeze five of them into a point at one end. Using a rounded modelling tool, press each into a fat petal shape. Arrange the five petals into a flower shape. ▶

3 Place the last ball in the flower centre and indent with a rounded modelling tool. For the fence, roll out and cut two strips each 1 cm/½ in wide to fit across the frame. Cut short strips for the posts. Trim the top of each post to a point. Construct the fence on greaseproof (waxed) paper.

4 For the leaves, roll out the clay, then cut basic leaf shapes and smooth out the edges with your fingers. Use a pointed modelling tool to trace a central vein on each one. Make 12 leaves in total.

5 Trace the templates provided for the pot and watering can and cut out. Cut out the shapes from clay, using the templates as a guide. Smooth the clay edges with your fingers.

6 For each three-dimensional pot, roll a ball of clay in your hand, then model it into a small pot shape. Let all the clay pieces dry on greaseproof paper for a few days.

7 Using an artist's paintbrush, paint the shapes in bright colours using acrylic paints, and allow to dry.

8 Use a glue gun to fix (attach) the picket fence and the other decorations to the chalk board frame.

DECORATED FLOWERPOTS

As terracotta pots age they acquire a beautiful patina of moss, algae and crystallized minerals, but brand new machine-made pots can also be given a unique personality with applied clay decorations. Here are some ideas

YOU WILL NEED
stiff cardboard, tracing paper and pencil
craft knife and cutting mat
terracotta modelling clay
rolling pin
terracotta pots
masking tape
wood glue
contour paste for ceramics or similar relief outliner
talcum powder, if needed
sharp knife
cake decorating cutters: bow, leaves etc (optional)
3 mm/⅛ in rolling guides
tape measure
scrap paper
craft moulds (optional)
acrylic or emulsion (latex) paints (optional)
medium artist's and small household paintbrushes (optional)
matt acrylic varnish (optional)

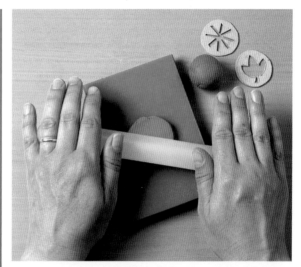

1 For each "wax seal" template, trace the design provided on to stiff cardboard. Cut out the central motif with a craft knife. Roll a small lump of clay into a ball and flatten slightly.

2 Firmly press the template into the clay, using the blunt edge of a knife to help deepen the impression through the holes. Carefully remove the template.

3 If the pot to be decorated is round, use masking tape to attach the motif to the pot so that the clay will dry with rounded sides.

4 When the clay motif is completely dry, stick it firmly to the pot using wood glue.

5 For the square "seal", cut a piece of stiff cardboard to shape and decorate with contour paste, following the template or your own design. Allow to dry thoroughly.

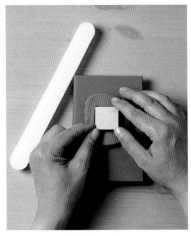

6 Roll out a small amount of clay. To stop the seal from sticking to the clay, dust the seal surface lightly with talcum powder. Press the seal into the clay. Remove carefully.

7 Cut around the motif with a sharp knife and tape to the pot to dry. Stick in place with wood glue.

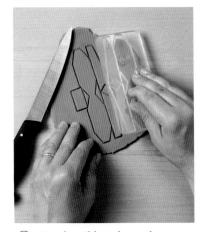

8 For the ribbon bow, draw a bow design freehand or use a cake decorating cutter. Roll out some clay to 3 mm/⅛in thick. Press the cutter firmly into the clay, then remove the excess. Neaten any rough edges.

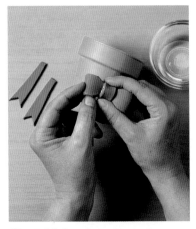

9 Fold the pieces into a bow shape and attach the "knot" piece by folding it over the front of the bow.

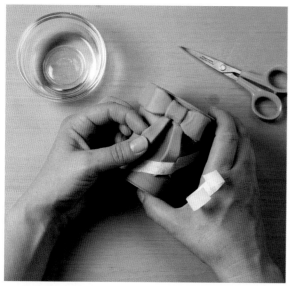

10 Moisten the clay to stick the pieces together, then arrange the bow on the pot. Lift the ribbon ends slightly. Secure with masking tape until dry enough to glue in place.

11 For the scalloped cuff, measure the circumference of the top of the pot then draw the cuff on paper to fit the pot.

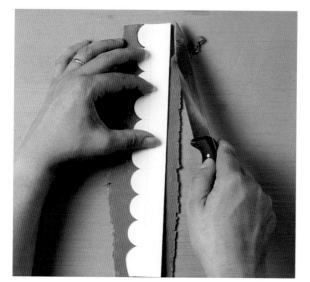

12 Roll out a length of clay 3 mm/⅛ in thick. Place the paper template on top and cut out with the sharp knife. Neaten any rough edges with the flat edge of a knife.

13 Place the cuff around the rim of the pot. Moisten the edges to join them neatly. Work some clay over the join with your fingers to tidy it up and secure with masking tape. Allow to dry with the pot upside down. ▶

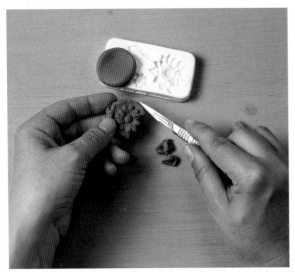

14 Craft moulds and cake decorating cutters can be used to make relief designs. Press clay into the mould, then cut out with a sharp knife, either cutting all around the detail or making it into a square or rectangular motif. You can combine several motifs on one pot.

15 Some motifs, such as oak leaves or small daisies, look good when repeated. Paint the pots with acrylic paints, or for large areas, use emulsion (latex); terracotta is porous and will absorb a lot of paint. Protect with several coats of varnish.

ROSE DRAWER HANDLES

Beautiful, realistic-looking roses form the handles on a decorative set of small drawers
in which to keep little treasures. The edges are painted to match the flowers, and the
drawer fronts are given a charming crackle-glaze finish.

YOU WILL NEED

paste food colouring or acrylic paints in pink and green
cocktail sticks (toothpicks)
white modelling clay
rolling pin
rose petal and calyx cake decorating cutters
plastic food wrap
balling tool (optional)
sharp knife
small wooden chest of drawers
fine sandpaper
acrylic primer or emulsion (latex) paint
artist's paintbrush
crackle-effect base coat
newspaper
crackle glaze in dark cream
masking tape
matt acrylic varnish
varnish brush
wood glue

1 Colour two balls of clay, one with pink and one
with green food colouring or acrylic paints (see
Basic Techniques). Add a small amount of colour to
the clay, then fold the clay around the colour. Roll
the clay between the palms of your hands into a
sausage shape. Fold the ends to the middle and
roll again. Repeat until all the colour is evenly
distributed. The colour will alter as the clay dries.

2 To make the rose centre, roll a small cone in pink
clay. Indent it at the wider end so that it will
stand on its own small base. If you are making several
roses, make them at the same time so that if you run
out of coloured clay, they will all share the colour
variations that may exist.

3 For the petals, roll out quite thinly a small amount of the pink clay. Take the small round cutter and press out two or three petals.

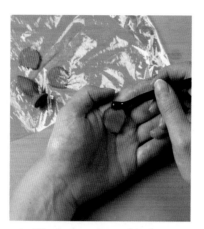

4 Pinch the edges of each petal between your finger and thumb to make them fine, or use a ball tool to shape the petals. Cover the petals not in use with polythene (plastic) to stop them drying out.

5 Moisten the cone and gently wrap a petal around it. Wrap the second petal opposite the first and overlapping it. Curl the edges back slightly with your fingers.

6 Cut out three or four medium-sized petals and cup them as before, curling the edges slightly before wrapping them around the flower. Open out the tops a little.

7 Cut out at least four larger petals and cup them slightly more than the previous petals. Fit them slightly lower than the previous layer and give them a more pronounced backward curl.

8 Use a sharp knife to trim away the stand made under the pink cone. Roll out thinly some green clay and cut out the calyx. Moisten the calyx and sit the rose inside it, arranging the calyx to curl very slightly away from the rose. Allow to dry thoroughly. ▶

9 To prepare the chest of drawers, sand any rough edges before applying a coat of primer or emulsion (latex) paint. Leave to dry thoroughly.

10 Spray the drawers with the crackle-effect base coat. Allow to dry for at least one hour. Spray with crackle glaze, following the manufacturer's instructions. Mask off each side as you work around the sides of the drawers to stop the paint spattering on finished work.

11 Paint the insides and edges of the drawers pink to match the colour of the roses. Allow to dry.

12 Apply several coats of matt acrylic varnish to the roses to help the clay harden. Stick the roses on to the drawers with wood glue.

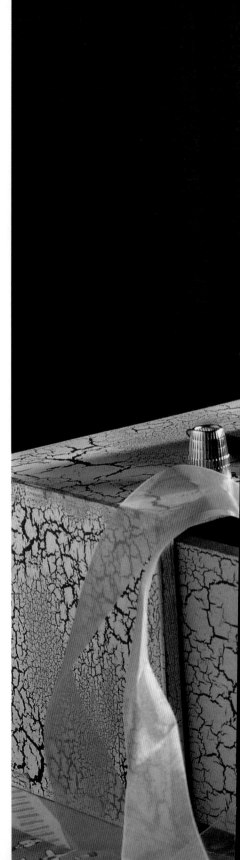

GILDED CURTAIN TIE-BACKS

These opulent golden tie-backs with an old-world feel will harmonize perfectly with the grandest curtains — no one would guess their humble origins as two plain wooden doorknobs and a ball of modelling clay.

YOU WILL NEED

tracing paper and pencil for templates
powdered clay hardener
modelling clay
polythene (plastic) bag
3 mm/⅛ in rolling guides
rolling pin
large and small cup or glass to use as circular templates
sharp knife
modelling tool
scrap paper
PVA (white) glue
paintbrush
red oxide acrylic paint
wooden flat-topped doorknob
fine sandpaper
wood glue
acrylic gold size
Dutch metal leaf in gold
soft brush
acrylic gloss varnish

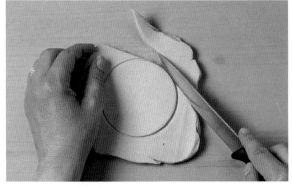

1 Mix the hardener into the clay (see Basic Techniques). Keep any clay not in use covered with a polythene (plastic) bag. To make the circular base for each tie-back, roll a piece of clay 3 mm/⅛ in thick and mark a circle with the large template. This will be the diameter of the finished tie-back. Cut out with a sharp knife. Smooth any fibrous edges.

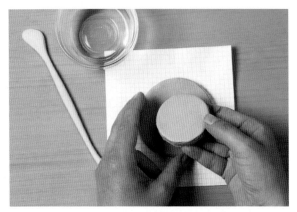

2 Roll a piece of clay 1 cm/½ in thick. Use the small template to cut a circle. Position this on top of the first circle and place both on a sheet of paper on which you can leave the finished work to dry.

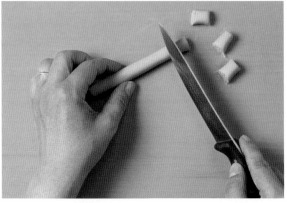

3 Evenly roll out a sausage of clay and cut it into sections with a sharp knife. Make all the pieces the same size.

4 Roll each piece into a ball sufficiently large to sit higher than the central circle when positioned on the large circle. Place each around the outside of the central circle, moistening the clay to help it stick. Indent each with the blunt side of the knife.

5 Make a second set of balls in the same way, this time rolling a slightly thinner sausage and cutting it into smaller sections. Place these around the edge of the small circle. These sit higher than the first row.

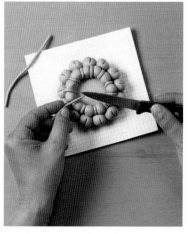

6 Roll some very thin sausages to position over the joins between the smaller clay balls. Arrange them in position and cut away the excess with the sharp knife. Tuck the ends through the gap between the balls as you work.

7 To make the centre, roll a ball of clay and flatten it slightly. Place this in the centre of the tie-back.

8 Make a tiny cone of clay to sit on the top of the flattened circle: pinch it with your fingers until you have the right shape. Moisten the clay and stick it on top.

9 Make a final set of smaller balls. Place these all around the central motif and score them with the blunt edge of the knife. Leave the clay to dry out completely. ▶

10 Paint the tie-back with two coats of PVA (white) glue, so that everything adheres. When dry, paint all over with red oxide acrylic paint.

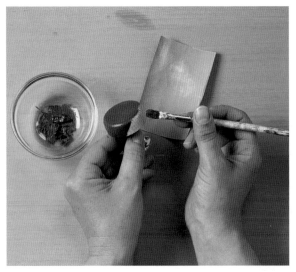

11 Rub down the doorknob with fine sandpaper, then paint it with red oxide. Apply several generous coats.

12 Stick the doorknob to the back of the tie-back with wood glue. Allow to dry.

13 Apply a coat of acrylic gold size over the tie-back. When the size is tacky, apply the Dutch metal leaf. Gently place a leaf over the clay and tap it down with a soft dry brush. Cover any bare areas only after the first layer has dried completely. Finish by applying four coats of acrylic gloss varnish.

HEN MESSAGE BOARD

This terracotta hen is constructed from layers of clay to give a three-dimensional effect. Set against a simple background of unfinished, natural wood slats, it makes a lovely wall decoration for a rustic-style kitchen.

YOU WILL NEED

pencil	wooden fruit crate
scissors	screwdriver
3 mm/⅛ in rolling guides	saw
rolling pin	panel pins (thumbtacks)
terracotta modelling clay	hammer
sharp knife	picture hook (optional)
modelling tool	liquid clay hardener
rigid sheets of cardboard	paintbrushes
masking tape	matt acrylic varnish
weight, if needed	varnish brush
wood glue	small hooks

1 Enlarge the templates provided to the required size. Make a template for each of the sections that build up into layers for the hen; number them if you find this helpful.

2 Roll out the clay to 3 mm/ ⅛ in thick. Place the first paper template on the clay and cut around the shape with a sharp knife. Repeat for each template.

3 Smooth the edges of the three wing sections with a modelling tool to neaten them. Attach each piece to a rigid surface with masking tape to prevent the clay from distorting as it dries.

4 To make the legs, use the shape of the feet on the largest template as a guide. Form the legs and toes with sausage shapes. Carefully position each on the background template. Moisten the clay with water to make the legs stick.

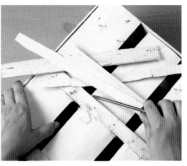

5 Model the details around the head and the comb using small pieces of clay. Moisten the clay to help it stick in place. Roll small sausages for the feathers around the legs. Use masking tape to secure the clay to a flat surface while drying and if necessary use a small weight to keep the body flat.

6 On the second body add an eye using a tiny ball. Model the beak from a small cone. Roll small sausages for the neck feathers. Arrange them in rows starting from the bottom and working upwards in layers. You may need to use a little glue at this stage. Use the point of the knife to align the feathers. Allow to dry thoroughly.

7 To make the board background, carefully dismantle the wooden crate using a screwdriver. Saw the wide slats to a uniform length for the background, then cut four more lengths to make a frame.

8 To construct the board, join the wide pieces with wood glue. Use masking tape to hold the board firm until it dries. Cut the frame pieces to size. Attach them to the background with panel pins (thumbtacks). Glue a hook on the back.

9 When the clay is dry, paint the pieces with liquid clay hardener, then follow with several coats of matt acrylic varnish.

10 Carefully assemble the hen in layers, sticking the pieces firmly together with wood glue. Attach small hooks around the frame to finish.

SUMMER VASE

To give a room an instant splash of Mediterranean sunshine, transform a plain ceramic vase with bright yellow enamel paint and a boldly painted relief design of lavender sprigs – the essence of Provence.

YOU WILL NEED
ceramic vase
quick-drying yellow enamel paint
medium and fine paintbrushes
modelling clay
pointed modelling tool
acrylic paints in green and lavender
clear enamel spray

1 Wash and dry the vase to remove grease and dust. Apply a coat of yellow enamel paint and allow to dry. Paint on another coat if necessary to achieve an even coverage.

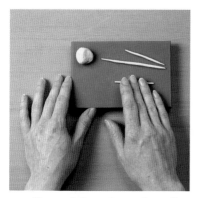

2 For each lavender sprig, roll a small ball of clay into one long thin sausage and two shorter ones; these will form the stem and leaves.

3 Using a paintbrush, apply a wide stripe of yellow enamel paint where you intend to put a lavender sprig. This glues the clay in place while it dries.

4 Carefully press the stalk into position on the vase.

▶

5 Flatten the smaller sausages to resemble long thin leaves and position them on each side of the stem, close to the base. To make each flower, roll a tiny piece of clay into a ball. Press each tiny ball to the top of the flower stem.

6 Using a pointed modelling tool, make an indentation in the base of each flower. Make several flower stems in this way and place them at random all over the vase. Set aside overnight for the clay to dry completely.

7 Using acrylic paints and a fine paintbrush, colour the lavender sprigs and leave to dry.

8 Protect the finished vase with a coat of clear enamel spray.

BACCHUS GARDEN PLAQUE

Set a convivial tone for summer parties in the garden by hanging
this terracotta relief on the wall. The genial god of wine can smile benignly
down on the proceedings.

YOU WILL NEED
pencil
tracing paper
scissors
5 mm/¼ in rolling guides
rolling pin
modelling clay
sharp knife
hatpin or tapestry needle
modelling tools
5 cm/2 in strong wire
wire cutters
acrylic craft paints in red oxide and cream
medium artist's paintbrushes
spray matt varnish

1 Enlarge the template provided to 25 cm/10 in
wide at its widest point. Trace the outline and
details and cut out. Roll out a slab of clay the same
size as the template and 5 mm/¼ in thick. Place the
tracing on the clay and cut around it.

2 Use a hatpin to transfer the details on to the clay,
by making a series of pinpricks along each line.
Peel off the paper and smooth the edges.

3 Draw in the features with a pointed modelling tool, using the pin pricks as a guide.

4 Make the hair from small sausages and coils of clay pressed gently along the guidelines. Use a flat-ended modelling tool to emphasize the shapes between the curls.

5 Roll out the remaining clay to a thickness of 5 mm/¼ in. Transfer the leaves from the tracing. Cut them out and press into place on the guidelines. Use a modelling tool to make the veins in the leaves.

6 Make small balls for the grapes and press into place, moistening the clay if necessary to help it stick. Make the beard in the same way as the hair, with coils and spirals of clay.

7 Press a loop of wire into the back to make a hanger for the plaque, then leave the plaque to dry completely.

8 Combine red oxide and cream paint to make a deep terracotta shade. Paint the plaque and allow it to dry thoroughly.

9 For a more weathered, textured effect, add another coat of red oxide paint, applied with a dry brush to give a stippled result.

10 Add some highlights with a little cream paint, stippled on to the hair and beard with a dry brush. Spray on several coats of matt varnish to make the plaque weatherproof.

SILVER-LEAF FINIALS

Give a plain wooden curtain pole a flourish at each end. These silvered finials look like intricate carved wood and make a beautiful finishing touch at the window. The pole and fittings can be decorated in silver to match.

YOU WILL NEED
bradawl
2 small metal screwtop lids
wood glue
2 small wood screws
2 x 7.5 cm/3 in lengths of
wooden dowel, each
1 cm/½ in diameter
screwdriver
stiff cardboard
craft knife
metal ruler
cutting mat
tinfoil
modelling clay

modelling tools
tracing paper and pencil
scissors
sharp knife
turquoise acrylic or
emulsion (latex) paint
paintbrushes
curtain pole and fittings
acrylic size
stencil brush
Dutch metal leaf in silver
soft brush
spray acrylic varnish
epoxy resin glue

1 Pierce a small hole through the centre of each screwtop with a bradawl. Using wood glue and a small wood screw, attach each screwtop lid to a length of dowel. Allow the glue to set hard.

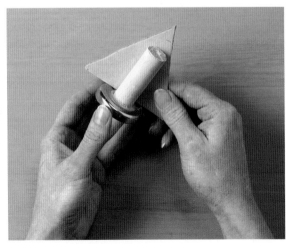

2 Cut a triangle for each finial from stiff cardboard and glue to the back of each dowel.

3 Take a piece of tinfoil, crumple it a little and then wrap it around the dowel and the cardboard to make a smooth shape.

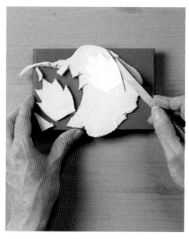

4 Break off small pieces of modelling clay and cover the entire shape with a thin layer. Use your fingers or a flat modelling tool to smooth out the surface of the clay. Repeat for the second finial.

5 Roll small balls of clay in the palm of your hand. Press each one lightly to the top of the pointed shape in close overlapping rows. Use a pointed modelling tool to make an indentation in the base of each one.

6 Trace and enlarge the leaf template provided. Cut out three leaves from a flattened piece of clay for each finial.

7 Wrap the leaves around the berry-covered centre piece and press the base of each securely on to the clay. Curl the tip of each leaf outwards. Repeat for the second finial.

8 Using a pointed modelling tool, lightly trace the veins on each leaf into the surface of the clay.

9 Roll two small balls of clay into a tapered sausage. Roll up the tapered end and press the other end to the base of the finial. Use modelling tools to smooth out any unsightly joins at the base. Leave the finials to dry for a few days. ▶

10 Apply one or two coats of turquoise acrylic or emulsion (latex) paint to the finials, the curtain pole and fittings. Allow to dry thoroughly after each coat.

11 Apply a mottled coat of acrylic size using a stencil brush. Leave to become slightly tacky.

12 Apply the silver leaf one sheet at a time, tapping down gently with a soft dry brush. Make sure that there are no draughts in your work space as the leaf is very light and delicate and will blow away. The leaf will adhere unevenly allowing the coloured paint to show through.

13 With the same dry brush, gently remove all loose flakes of leaf. Brush the surface firmly to make sure that the silver leaf has adhered. Seal all surfaces with one or two coats of varnish and allow to dry completely. Glue the finials to the ends of the curtain pole with epoxy resin glue.

GEOMETRIC PICTURE FRAMES

These pure white frames are co-ordinated yet individually decorated. Restrained,
geometric relief designs add interest with the play of light and shadow,
yet do not overwhelm the contents of the frames.

YOU WILL NEED
3 mm/⅛ in rolling guides
rolling pin
white modelling clay
small round and square metal cutters (cookie cutters)
cocktail stick (toothpick)
sharp knife and ruler, if necessary
round-ended knife
masking tape
plain wooden picture frames
fine sandpaper
white acrylic or emulsion (latex) paint
paintbrush
emery board
wood glue
matt acrylic varnish

1 Roll out a small piece of clay to an even
thickness of about 3 mm/⅛ in. Using the round
cutter, cut out several shapes from the clay.

2 Pierce the centre of each clay disc with a cocktail
stick (toothpick) and allow to dry.

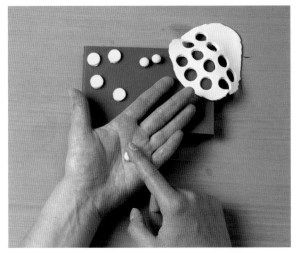

3 For an alternate design, cut out a number of clay discs as before. Roll each disc in the palm of your hand, then between your fingers to make more spherical, evenly sized balls. Allow the balls to dry thoroughly.

4 For the squares, roll out the clay, then cut out small squares using a square cutter. (Use a sharp knife with a ruler as a guide if you do not have a cutter.) Decorate with several different marks: single holes, straight lines, using the flat end of a knife, and a combination of both. Aim to have about five different designs. Adhere each to a flat surface with masking tape so that the edges do not curl. Allow to dry.

5 To prepare the frames, first sand each gently to provide a key for the paint, then apply several coats of white acrylic or emulsion (latex) paint.

6 File any rough edges from the clay motifs using an emery board. Arrange the motifs on the frames, experimenting with different combinations until you are satisfied. Stick in place with wood glue. ▶

39

7 When the glue is dry, apply one or two coats of white paint to the entire frame, followed by several coats of matt acrylic varnish. Allow each coat to dry before applying the next.

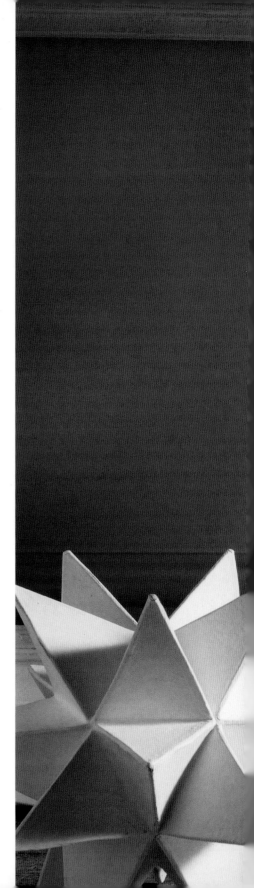

LEAF WALL PLAQUES

Achieve a lovely three-dimensional effect by impressing a simple cardboard template in a flat slab of soft clay. The cut-out details are given depth by hidden spacers that hold each plaque away from the wall.

YOU WILL NEED

tracing paper and pencil	scissors
cardboard for template	fine wire
craft knife	wire cutters
cutting mat	wood glue
hardener (optional)	emery board or fine sandpaper
modelling clay	PVA (white) glue
1 cm/½ in rolling guides	paintbrush
rolling pin	acrylic paints
sharp knife	matt acrylic varnish
paper	

1 Using the template provided, cut a leaf design from cardboard. Mix the clay hardener into the clay. Using rolling guides, roll out a slab of clay to a depth of about 1 cm/½ in. Position the template on the clay and press it gently and evenly down so that clay protrudes through the holes. Use the knife to help.

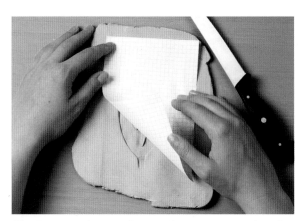

2 Remove the template. Make a paper template for the plaque shape. Place it very lightly on the clay, and cut out the plaque using a sharp knife.

3 Carefully cut out the leaf veins from the clay. Smooth the edges of the plaque with the flat edge of the knife. Allow the clay to dry completely. ▶

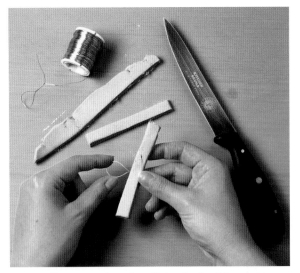

4 Roll out two lengths of clay for backing strips. Cut a short piece of wire and insert it into the top of one strip, taking care to arrange the loop so that it will not be seen when the plaque is hanging. If you are making a set of plaques, make sure all the wires are an equal length.

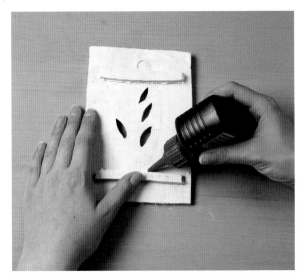

5 When the plaque and strips are dry, stick the strips to the back of the plaque using wood glue. One strip should be across the top of the plaque, and another across the bottom.

6 File or sand the edges of the clay very gently to remove burrs. Paint the entire plaque with two coats of PVA (white) glue to seal the clay and help prevent chipping.

7 Add a coat of acrylic paint. Then paint the indented leaf a slightly darker shade of the main colour. Seal with several coats of matt acrylic varnish, allowing it to dry between coats.

FLORAL LINEN SCENTERS

Because clay is porous it can be scented with your favourite essential oil and it will hold the perfume beautifully for weeks. These pretty floral motifs will keep your own clothes smelling sweet; they also make superb presents.

YOU WILL NEED

tracing paper and pencil
scissors
3 mm/⅛ in rolling guides
rolling pin
modelling clay
sharp knife
modelling tool
essential oil
wire cutters
wire coathanger
pliers
rigid sheet of cardboard
masking tape
small flower cutters (for cake decorating)
cocktail stick (toothpick)
fine wire
wood glue
jam jar
acrylic gouache
paintbrush
matt acrylic varnish
ribbon

1 Enlarge the template provided to the required size and cut out. Roll out the clay evenly, to a depth of about 3 mm/⅛ in. Place the template on the clay and cut around the shape with a sharp knife.

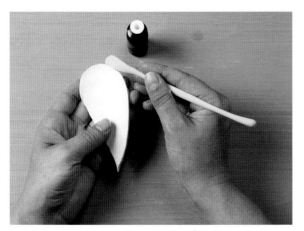

2 Tidy the edges of the clay with the modelling tool. Sprinkle on a few drops of essential oil.

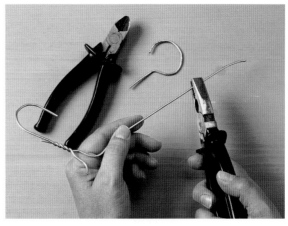

3 Cut a short length from a wire coathanger, using wire cutters. Shape with pliers into a neat hook. ▶

45

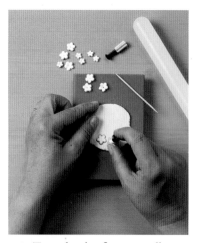

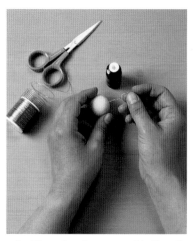

4 Gently push at least 2.5 cm/ 1 in of the hook into the top of the clay. Secure on a rigid surface with masking tape to keep the clay flat, and allow to dry.

5 To make the flowers, roll out a thin piece of clay. Using a flower cutter, cut out the required number of flowers. Carefully pierce the centres with a cocktail stick (toothpick). Allow to dry.

6 To make the scented ball, roll a piece of clay into a sphere in the palm of your hand. Insert a very small loop of fine wire deep into the clay. Sprinkle with essential oil. Allow to dry.

7 Stick the flowers to the motifs using wood glue. Work around the ball in sections. Suspend the ball by the wire loop from a cocktail stick over a jar to dry. Add more essential oil as desired.

8 When the flowers are dry, check that the hook is firmly in place: use glue to secure it if necessary. Paint the motifs with acrylic gouache, dabbing the paint into the crevices. Begin with a dark shade, then brush a lighter shade on to the raised surfaces with a dry brush. Apply a coat of matt acrylic varnish.

9 To cover the hook with ribbon, leave an end to tie in a bow and work up the hook from the motif to the cut end of wire, then back again. Finish by tying the ends of the ribbon in a bow. Refresh the clay from time to time with essential oil, but make sure it is dry before hanging it next to clothing.

MOSAIC MIRROR

The organic, freeform shape of this mirror frame is inspired by the pliable nature of the clay, but enlivened by the sharp contrast of angular shards of glossy tiles and opalescent beads embedded into the clay while it is still soft.

YOU WILL NEED
assorted ceramic tiles
2 mirror tiles each 15 cm/6 in square
old towel
hammer
scissors
1 cm/½ in and 8 mm/⅜ in rolling guides
rolling pin
modelling clay
sharp knife
fruit corer
wire for hanging
8 beads
fine sandpaper
acrylic gesso
pink acrylic paint
paintbrushes

1 Wrap the ceramic tiles and one of the mirror tiles in an old towel. Hit with a hammer to break the tiles randomly into mosaic pieces.

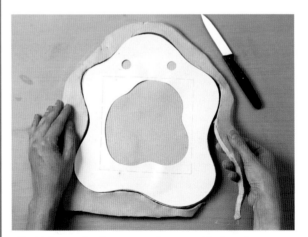

2 Enlarge the frame template provided and cut out. Cut out the hanging holes and central opening. Roll out a piece of clay 1 cm/½ in thick for the mirror back. Place the template on top and cut around it. Pull away the excess clay.

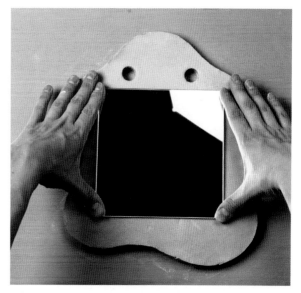

3 Punch out the hanging holes using a fruit corer. Do not cut away the clay in the centre of the mirror. Remove the template.

4 Position the remaining mirror tile on the clay using the broken lines on the template as a guide. Press the mirror into the clay. Thread the hanging wire through the holes and secure at the back. Press the clay over the wire at the front.

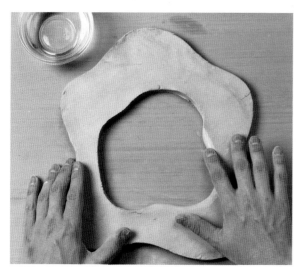

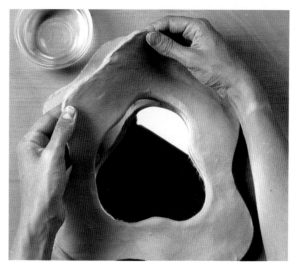

5 Roll a second piece of clay 8 mm/⅜ in thick for the front of the frame. Place the template on top and cut around the circumference and the central opening. Pull away the excess clay. Smooth the edges of the opening with a moistened finger.

6 Carefully lift the clay front and place it over the mirror tile and the back, matching the outer edges. Smooth the outer edges with a moistened finger to blend the seam and the cut edges.

▶

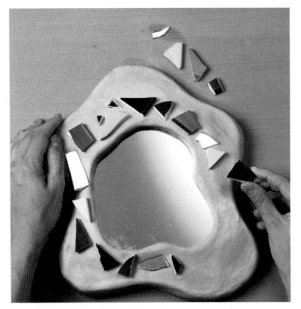

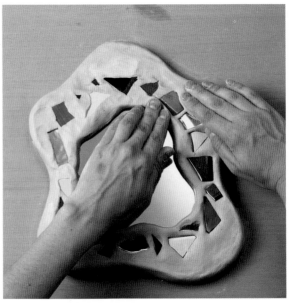

7 Moisten the top of the clay. Arrange the mosaic pieces around the mirror.

8 Press the mosaic pieces into the clay. Then press the clay over the edges of the pieces to secure.

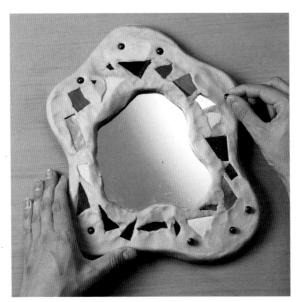

9 Arrange the beads on the frame, then embed them into the clay. Leave the mirror to harden completely. If any cracks appear in the clay around the mosaic pieces, add more moistened clay and leave to harden.

10 Lightly sand the outer edges. Undercoat the mirror with acrylic gesso. Paint the clay frame pink. Use a fine brush to paint around the edges of the mirror tile, the mosaic pieces and beads.

TEXTURED LAMP BASE

*The gourd-like shape and surface texture of this lamp base are achieved
by pressing small pieces of rolled clay onto a papier-mâché and wire armature.
The sponged painting technique accentuates its tactile quality.*

YOU WILL NEED
long-nosed pliers
chicken wire
tape measure
short length of 2.5 cm/1 in diameter dowel
medium- and fine-gauge galvanized wire
newspaper
wallpaper paste
modelling clay
rolling pin
acrylic paints in cream, yellow, orange and red
paintbrush
natural sponge
bottle lamp fitting and flex (cord)

1 Using pliers, cut a rectangle of chicken wire
about 15 x 19 cm/6 x 7½ in. Turn in one long
edge for extra strength. Roll the short end around a
length of dowel to form a cylinder for the neck.

2 Cut another rectangle of chicken wire about
30 x 45 cm/12 x 18 in and bend it to form a
cylinder, twisting the ends of the wire together
to make a neat seam. Use the pliers to pinch the
chicken wire together a little at one end: this will
form the bottom edge of the lamp base.

3 Bend a length of medium-gauge galvanized wire
into a circle about 10 cm/4 in in diameter, and
bind with fine-gauge wire all the way around.

4 Place the wire ring inside the bottom of the cylinder, fold the ends of the chicken wire over the ring and, using the fine wire, "stitch" the ring securely in place.

5 Use the pliers to pinch the chicken wire, working slowly, row by row, to make the cylinder into a smooth pear shape.

6 Slide the neck piece into the top of the wire shape and bind in place with fine-gauge galvanized wire, as before.

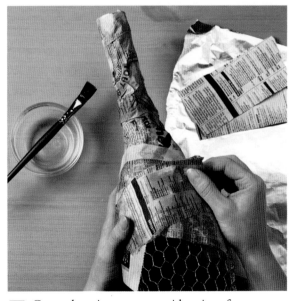

7 Cover the wire armature with strips of newspaper soaked in wallpaper paste to make a smoother surface. Leave for a few days to dry hard. ▶

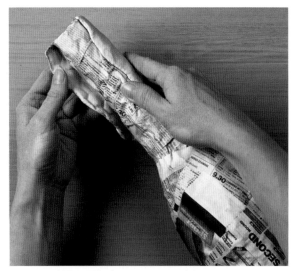

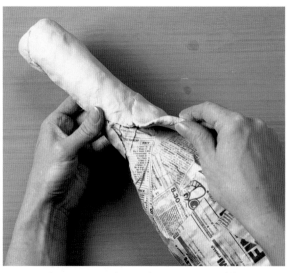

8 Cover the dry armature with clay, beginning at the neck. Roll out slabs of clay to a thickness of about 1 cm/½ in. Place each on the armature, smoothing out the joins (seams) with your fingers.

9 Work your way down the armature, adding rolled-out sections of clay until it is completely covered. Pierce a hole near the base for the flex (cord). Leave the lamp base to dry out completely.

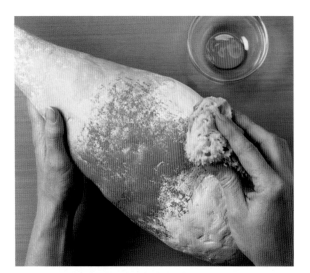

10 Paint the top half of the lamp base with one or two coats of cream acrylic paint, allowing each coat to dry before applying the next. Using a small natural sponge, apply a mottled band of yellow paint, blending to orange lower down. Apply a mottled band of red paint blending to a solid colour at the bottom.

11 Put the flex (cord) through the top of the lamp base and out through the hole at the bottom, then push the lamp fitting into the neck. It should fit quite snugly, but if necessary, use a little clay to fill in any gaps.

ROCOCO WALL PLAQUE

A rough-cast plaster finish enlivens a plain interior wall but you can add more texture and decorative interest by applying clay motifs directly to the wall before painting it. Highlight the details with white as a finishing touch.

YOU WILL NEED
tracing paper and pencil
scissors
masking tape
permanent marker pen
8 mm/⅜ in and 5 mm/¼ in rolling guides
rolling pin
modelling clay
sharp knife
wood glue
fine and medium paintbrushes
fruit corer
drinking straw
blue emulsion (latex) paint
white emulsion paint
PVA (white) glue

1 Enlarge the templates provided for the motifs to a suitable size. Cut each out of paper. Tape the plaque template B to a coarsely plastered wall and draw carefully around the outline with a permanent marker pen. Remove the template then draw around motifs A in the same way.

2 Roll the clay out to a thickness of 8 mm/⅜ in. Cut out motif A using a sharp knife. Smooth the cut edges with the flat edge of a knife.

3 On the wall, spread wood glue inside motif A and up to the drawn lines.

4 Carefully press the clay motif A on to the wall over the drawn motif. Smooth along the edges with a moistened finger.

5 Roll out another piece of clay to a thickness of 5 mm/¼ in. Cut out the relief pieces for motif A. Moisten the undersides and press in position. Pat the cut edges with a moistened finger to round them.

6 Indent the details on the clay using the handle of a fine paintbrush.

▶

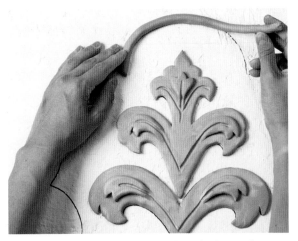

7 Roll sausages of clay 1 cm/½in thick. Apply a line of glue to the wall along one section of the plaque outline. Press the sausage on top. Cut off the excess clay at the angled points. Repeat until the plaque outline is complete.

8 Roll out some clay to a thickness of 5 mm/¼in. Stamp nine circles using a fruit corer. Gently roll each circle between your fingers to smooth the sides. Indent the centres of all the circles using a drinking straw. Dab a little glue on the underside of each and press three circles to the wall below the point of motif B. Press the remaining circles to the plaque outline at the corners.

9 Roll six 1.5 cm/⅝in diameter balls of clay for the leaves. Mould each ball between your fingers to form a flattened leaf shape. Indent a vein along the centre with the handle of a fine paintbrush. Dab wood glue on the undersides and press each leaf on to the plaque outline.

10 When the clay is completely dry, paint the plaque with PVA (white) glue followed when dry by two coats of blue emulsion (latex) paint. To finish, pick out the plaque details in white emulsion paint as desired.

FLORENTINE BOXES

Formalized leaves and gilded scroll-work turn simple square boxes into encrusted Renaissance treasures. You could line the inside of each with sumptuous fabric to hold jewellery or mementoes, or to display a very special gift.

YOU WILL NEED

square and rectangular cardboard craft boxes
tracing paper
hard and soft pencils
masking tape
ball-point pen
modelling clay
modelling tools
PVA (white) glue
medium and fine paintbrushes
acrylic craft paints in white, pale lilac and pale blue
dark and pale gold metallic paint
matt acrylic spray varnish

1 Enlarge the templates provided to fit the top and sides of the box lid. Trace the outline with a hard pencil, then rub over the reverse with a soft pencil. Tape the paper to the lid. Draw over the lines again using a ball-point pen.

2 Make the four leaf shapes from small rolls of clay and press them into position on the box lid. Use modelling tools to add the details, and smooth the clay with a damp finger.

3 Make the dots from small balls of clay. Press them in place with the point of a pencil.

4 Finish the design on top of the lid by adding the four trefoil motifs on the corners.

5 Make the scrolls and leaves for each side of the lid. Allow the clay to dry thoroughly.

6 Paint the lid with PVA (white) glue diluted with an equal quantity of water. Paint the lid and box with white acrylic paint.

7 Paint the lid with a base coat of pale lilac.

8 Add a stippling of pale blue paint, applied with an almost dry brush.

9 Using a fine brush, paint the motifs in dark gold. When dry, add pale gold highlights as desired.

10 Give a textured look to the lid by brushing over the surface with a dry brush loaded with a small amount of gold paint.

11 Paint the bottom of the box to match, adding a small amount of gold paint to each edge. Finish by spraying the box and lid with a protective coat of matt varnish.

MEXICAN CANDLESTICKS

Bright, hot colours give a carnival feel to these pretty candlesticks shaped like exotic desert flowers. The base of each is simply made from balls of clay stacked on top of each other, taking care to keep the sticks straight while they dry.

YOU WILL NEED
rolling pin
modelling clay
7.5 cm/3 in diameter glass
sharp knife
modelling tool
cocktail sticks (toothpicks)
candles
knitting needle
acrylic craft paints in pink, green, light and dark blue
paintbrushes
acrylic matt varnish

1 For each candlestick, roll out a piece of clay to a thickness of about 5 mm/¼ in. Use the rim of the glass to stamp a circle on it.

2 Cut out the disc using a sharp knife and neaten the edges using a modelling tool.

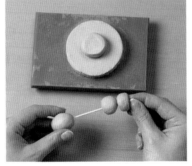

3 Press a 3 cm/1¼ in diameter ball of clay into the centre of the disc and flatten. Make a flat-tened 2 cm/¾ in ball, a 3 cm/1¼ in ball and an elongated 4 cm/1½ in ball, and thread them all on to a cocktail stick (toothpick). Press into the middle of the base.

4 Hollow out a ball of clay to fit the candle. To make small petals, roll out pea-sized balls of clay and flatten them. Press each to the rim of the candlestick cup for the decoration.

▶

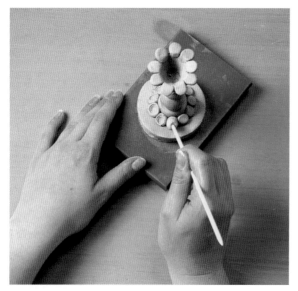

5 Make small balls of clay and press them in a ring around the base of the candlestick. Indent each with the top of a knitting needle.

6 Roll some more small balls to decorate the rim of the candlestick and the section between the cup and stem of the candlestick. Indent each with the point of the knitting needle.

7 Score a series of lines on the base, cup and elongated clay ball using a cocktail stick. Allow the candlestick to dry completely.

8 Paint the top petals and the round ball pink, the rings of dots green and the rest of the candlestick pale blue. Drag dark blue paint over the scored stripes for a two-colour effect. Individualize the candlestick as desired. Finish with several coats of matt varnish.

COIL POT

Long before the invention of the potter's wheel, craftsmen used to create vessels of great beauty and elegance, using this ancient coiling technique. It is still used by potters all over the world.

YOU WILL NEED
powdered clay hardener
modelling clay
polythene (plastic) bag
rolling pin
6 mm/¼ in rolling guides
cup or glass
sharp knife
modelling tool
PVA (white) glue
coarse and fine paintbrushes
water-based household paints in deep
powder blue, aqua and lime
scarlet acrylic gouache
matt acrylic varnish

1 Mix the hardener into the clay. Keep any clay not in use covered with a polythene (plastic) bag. To make the base of the bowl, roll out a circle of clay between rolling guides. Gently press a cup or glass into the clay to mark a circle the size you wish the base of the pot to be.

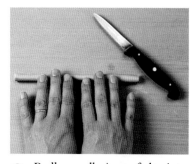

2 Roll a small piece of clay into a sausage. Keep the sausage as even as possible. The diameter of the coil will determine the thickness of the pot walls throughout the process.

3 Arrange the sausage over the indented base mark. Cut the ends at an angle to overlap them neatly. Smooth the join (seam) in the coil using a modelling tool.

4 The first coil must adhere to the base, so smooth the clay on to the base all around the inside of the coil, using your finger or the modelling tool.

5 Score the top of the first coil lightly with the tip of the sharp knife to help the next layer to adhere.

▶

6 Make a second coil in the same way. Place it on top of the first, making sure the join is in a different place from that of the first coil.

7 Using the modelling tool, smooth the coils together inside and outside as you make the pot walls. The modelling tool helps create texture, so experiment with different score-marks until you find one that suits the piece you are making.

8 As the pot gets taller, position each coil slightly to the edge of the one below to make the opening larger.

9 Cut away the excess clay around the base of the pot with the sharp knife. When you have finished the pot, smooth the top edge with the sharp knife or modelling tool. Allow the pot to dry completely.

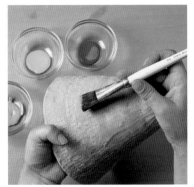

10 Seal the pot with PVA (white) glue, diluted with an equal quantity of water. Using a large, coarse brush, paint the outside of the pot with two or three shades of colour, brushing the paint on at random and build-ing up the layers of colour. Keep the brush quite dry so that the paint picks up the texture made with the modelling tool.

11 Paint the inside with a single colour to complement the outside. Finish by painting around the rim with scarlet acrylic gouache, or the bright shade of your choice. Varnish the pot with several coats of matt acrylic varnish.

STONE-EFFECT PLATTERS

These square dishes, each gently curved and raised by simple feet, have an exquisitely restrained, Japanese quality. They eschew fussy decoration, but their style is enhanced by the wonderful surface texture, reminiscent of finely-worked stone.

YOU WILL NEED
soft, porous cloth
plastic food container
polythene (plastic) bag
elastic band
powdered clay hardener
modelling clay
rolling pin
5 mm/¼ in rolling guides
hessian (burlap)
paper
scissors
ruler
sharp knife
masking tape
PVA (white) glue
medium artist's
paintbrush
emery board or fine sandpaper
fine sand
acrylic paints
acrylic matt varnish

1 To prepare the mould, stretch the soft, porous cloth over the top of the container and secure it with an elastic band. Make sure the fabric is not too taut, as you want to create a gentle curve to mould the clay into a dish shape.

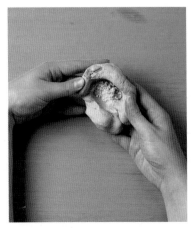

2 Knead the hardener into the clay. Keep any clay not in use in a polythene (plastic) bag.

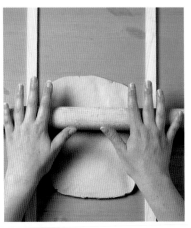

3 Roll out a slab of clay to an even thickness of 5 mm/¼ in, using rolling guides.

4 Place the hessian (burlap) on top and roll over it to make an impression in the clay.

5 Make a square template, measuring 12 cm/4½in. (For a large platter, make a 12 x 20 cm/4½ x 8 in template). Using the template, cut out the clay with a sharp knife.

6 Place the square carefully in the cloth mould and allow to dry thoroughly. This will give the clay a slightly scooped shape.

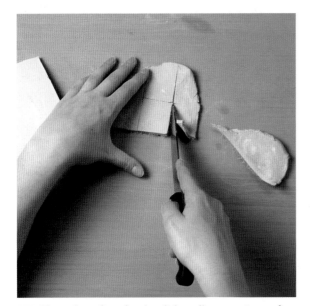

7 To make a foot for the dish, roll out a piece of clay to about 5 mm/¼in thick. Cut it into a 5 cm/2 in square using a sharp knife.

8 Place the foot on the underside of the dried dish and secure with masking tape. When dry, stick the foot in place with undiluted PVA (white) glue. ▶

9 File the raw edges of the platter to achieve a slightly rounded edge.

10 Paint the platter with two coats of PVA glue. While the second coat is still wet, sprinkle with fine sand. Allow the glue to dry before shaking off the excess sand. Repeat for a more textured look.

11 To coat the sides, paint with PVA glue, then dip into the sand and allow to dry before working on the underside. When you have achieved the desired effect, coat the whole platter with PVA.

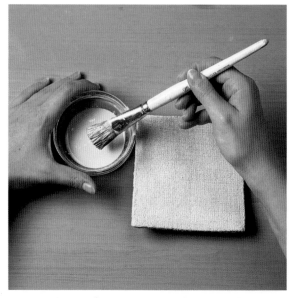

12 Mix acrylic paint to a sandy stone colour and paint the platter all over, adding more coats until the desired shade is reached. Seal with at least two coats of acrylic matt varnish.

FLEUR-DE-LYS WASTEBASKET

Emblazoned with elegant heraldic motifs, this pretty yet functional object is perfect
in a formal room. Painting it with a subtle mix of colours will give it an appearance of
antique metal, and enhance the relief effect of the clay decorations.

YOU WILL NEED
pencil
thin cardboard for template
scissors
5 mm/¼ in rolling guides
rolling pin
modelling clay
sharp knife
modelling tools
ruler
medium-density fibreboard (MDF) wastebasket
glue gun
acrylic paints in silver, dark grey, brown and cream
small household and medium
artist's paintbrushes
small sponge
spray matt varnish

1 Enlarge the template provided to 12.5 cm/5 in across. Transfer the outline on to thin cardboard and cut out. Roll out the clay to 5 mm/¼ in thick – you will need enough to make four fleurs-de-lys. Place the template on the clay and cut around the outside edge with a sharp knife.

2 Peel off the template and tidy the edges of the clay with a flat modelling tool or your finger.

3 Draw in the markings with a modelling tool, then allow the shapes to dry.

4 Draw two diagonals and a central vertical line on each side of the wastebasket.

5 Use the glue gun to glue the clay shapes carefully in place, making sure that they all line up. Keep your fingers away from the hot glue.

6 Paint the wastebasket and the fleur-de-lys motifs with silver paint. Allow to dry.

▶

7 Sponge on a thin layer of dark grey to look like galvanized metal.

8 Add some touches of brown paint, emphasizing the relief areas of the motifs.

9 With a dry brush, add small areas of cream paint to the motifs and wastebasket.

10 Finish off with several coats of spray matt varnish to protect the paintwork and motifs.

VERDIGRIS CLOCK

This delightful floral clock has no need of numerals: the twelve petals show the hours instead. The verdigris effect is achieved with clever use of paint, a technique which emphasizes the solidity of the sculpted design.

YOU WILL NEED
tracing paper
pencil
scissors
5 mm/¼ in rolling guides
rolling pin
modelling clay
sharp knife
hatpin or tapestry needle
modelling tools
ruler
clock mechanism with 7.5 cm/3 in hands
5 cm/2 in length of strong wire
glue gun
acrylic craft paints in bronze, mid-green, pale green and cream
medium and small artist's paintbrushes
varnish

1 Enlarge the template provided to measure 23 cm/9 in across and draw the outside petals and the inner circle separately on tracing paper. Cut out. Roll out a slab of clay 5 mm/¼ in thick, slightly larger than the main clock piece. Place the template on the clay. Cut out around the edge with a sharp knife.

2 Transfer the markings by pricking through the paper with a hatpin, then peel off the paper.

3 Use a flat modelling tool to emphasize these outlines and to give a three-dimensional shape to the petals. Smooth the clay as necessary.

4 Cut a square from the centre of the circle that is 1 cm/⅜in larger all around than the clock mechanism. Attach a hanging loop of wire to the back of the top petal.

5 Roll out a 15 cm/6 in diameter disc of clay for the clock centre. Cut out and transfer the markings to the clay as before, using the template.

6 Make a hole in the centre to fit the clock spindle, then shape around the dots and petals with a modelling tool to give a three-dimensional look.

7 Allow both pieces to dry completely, then glue them together with a glue gun.

▶

8 Paint the entire piece with a base coat of bronze acrylic craft paint. Allow to dry.

9 Brush on a coat of mid-green paint, allowing some of the bronze to show through.

10 Stipple on layers of pale green and cream with a dry brush. Paint with varnish to protect the surface.

11 Attach the clock mechanism, making sure that at 12.00 the hands line up with the wire hanger on the back of the finished piece.

MATERIALS

ACRYLIC VARNISH
This comes in matt, satin and gloss finishes, in liquid or aerosol form.

CLAY HARDENERS
Powdered hardeners harden the clay throughout; liquid hardeners seal and harden the outside only.

DUTCH METAL LEAF
Apply metal leaf for decoration.

GLUE
Use strong woodworking glue to stick clay to other surfaces and for repairs. Dilute PVA (white) glue with water for use as a sealant, or use alone.

HAND CREAM
Use when handling dry clay, to keep it moist.

MASKING TAPE
This is invaluable for keeping work in shape while it is drying.

MODELLING CLAY
There is a wide range of brands and qualities. Air-dried clay does not require firing, though you can strengthen some brands by baking or adding hardeners.

PAINT
Use acrylic artist's gouache for small projects, emulsion (latex) for large areas and for priming, and specialist paints for verdigris, crackle-glaze and metallic effects.

PAPER AND CARDBOARD
Use paper, tracing paper and cardboard for making templates. Tape clay to thick cardboard to dry flat.

PASTE FOOD COLOURING
Knead a small amount into clay. Concentrated ink or watercolour can also be used.

RELIEF OUTLINER
Apply straight from the tube to create embossing stamps.

SAND
Glue sand on to clay with PVA (white) glue for a textured effect.

TALCUM POWDER
Use on surfaces and cookie cutters to stop them sticking to the clay.

TILES
Embed pieces of broken tile in clay for a mosaic effect.

WIRE
Embed a wire hanging loop in the back of a piece. Use pliers to bend chicken wire to make an armature.

Opposite: acrylic varnish (1); clay hardener (2); Dutch metal leaf (3); glue (4); hand cream (5); masking tape (6); modelling clay (7); paper and cardboard (8); paint (9); paste food colouring (10); relief outliner (11); sand (12); talcum powder (13); tiles (14); wire (15); wood glue (16); hooks (17).

EQUIPMENT

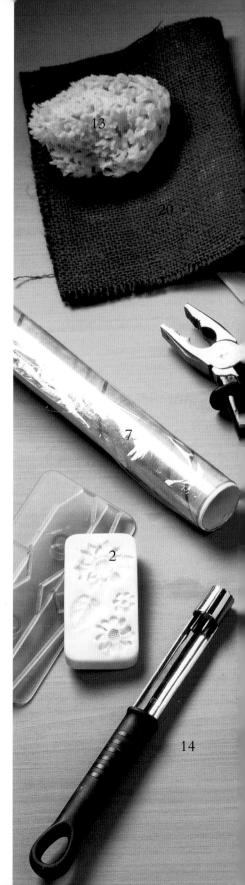

CUTTERS AND MOULDS
Cake decorating suppliers are a good source of flower and leaf moulds. Cocktail sticks (toothpicks), drinking straws and fruit corers make neat indentations.

HAMMER
Use a small lightweight hammer.

KNIVES AND SCISSORS
Use the blade of a sharp knife for cutting clay and the flat side for smoothing edges. Use a round-ended table knife for indenting, a craft knife for cardboard templates and delicate areas of clay, and scissors for paper templates.

MODELLING TOOLS
A wide variety are available, for shaping and smoothing clay. Use a balling tool to shape flower petals.

PAINTBRUSHES
Build up a collection in different shapes and sizes. Keep separate brushes for glue and varnish.

PENCIL
For tracing and marking designs.

PLASTIC WRAP AND POLYTHENE (PLASTIC) BAGS
Cover spare clay with plastic wrap or store inside a polythene (plastic) bag to keep it moist. Moisten the inside of the bag if necessary.

PLIERS AND WIRE CUTTERS
Use for forming armatures, bending and cutting wire for hooks.

ROLLING GUIDES
Use two strips of wood of an even depth on each side of the clay. Use as a guide to roll the clay evenly.

ROLLING PIN AND BOARD
Use a domestic rolling pin for large pieces of clay, and a small, cake decorator's rolling pin and non-stick board for small pieces.

SANDPAPER, NAIL FILES AND EMERY BOARDS
Use to smooth rough edges on dry clay before sealing or painting.

SAW
Use for cutting wood to size.

SPONGE
Use a small natural sponge to apply paint for a mottled effect.

Opposite: clay modelling tools (1); cutters and moulds (2); hammer (3); knives and scissors (4); paintbrushes (5); pencil (6); polythene (plastic) bags (7); pliers and wire cutters (8); rolling guides (9); rolling pins and board (10); sandpaper, emery board and nail files (11); saw (12); sponge (13); apple corer (14); nails (15); screwdriver (16); straw (17); cocktail sticks (toothpicks) (18); modelling knife (19); hessian (burlap) 20.

BASIC TECHNIQUES

Modelling clay is an easy subject to master. Once you have grasped the basics, you will quickly produce projects that you can be quite proud of.

MIXING CLAY WITH COLOUR

1 Use a concentrated colouring agent such as food colouring. Add gradually to achieve the shade required without making the clay too wet. The colour will dry a slightly different shade. Keep clay moist in polythene (plastic).

2 Roll the clay between your palms into a long sausage. Fold the ends to the middle and proceed to roll another sausage. Add more colour as necessary.

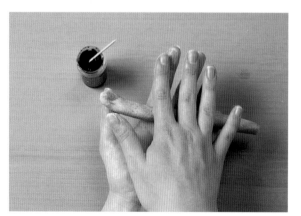

3 Repeat until all the colour is evenly distributed and you have achieved the desired shade.

USING HAND CREAM TO KEEP CLAY MOIST

Clay can dry out quickly, especially if the atmosphere is warm and dry. Always keep spare clay covered with plastic wrap or in a polythene (plastic) bag. It is useful to have some hand cream to mix into the clay to keep it moist. Do not add too much, as you do not want to make the clay unstable when dry.

MIXING CLAY WITH HARDENER

1 Make an indentation in the clay and add some powder hardener following the manufacturer's instructions. If you are using a liquid hardener, dilute as appropriate first. Fold the clay over the powder and knead a little before rolling into a sausage.

2 Fold the sausage in half and add more powder hardener. Repeat until you have used all the powder you need.

USING ROLLING GUIDES

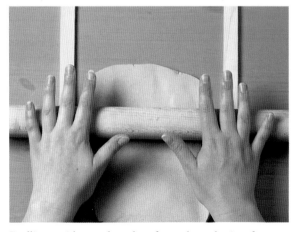

3 Knead the clay thoroughly to blend the hardener evenly into the clay. This treatment makes the clay more difficult to work with, so keep it moist in a polythene (plastic) bag and use hand cream to soften it while working.

Rolling guides are lengths of wood or plastic of a set depth. Place the guides at each side of the modelling clay to be rolled out and roll out the clay until the rolling pin sits on the guides. This method ensures that the clay is the same depth throughout.

ROLLING OUT CLAY

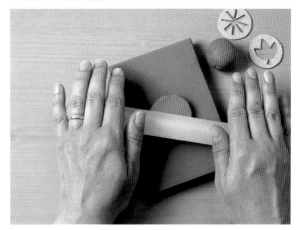

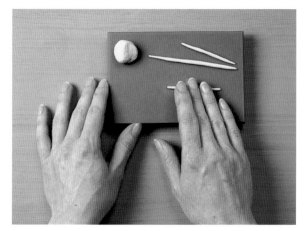

1 Work on a surface that can easily be wiped clean. A light dusting of talcum powder on the work surface and on the rolling pin helps prevent the clay from sticking. Take enough clay to complete the section you are working on. Flatten the clay with your hands then roll with the pin. Turn the clay around and keep rolling until you have a smooth, even slab.

2 A small non-stick rolling board and rolling pin designed for cake decorating are especially useful for rolling out small pieces of clay for delicate work.

CUTTING AROUND A TEMPLATE

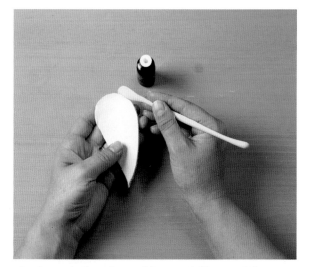

1 Some brands of modelling clay can be quite fibrous when cut, so neaten the edges with a modelling tool or the edge of a knife as you work. Moisten the tool slightly with water as necessary.

2 Smooth the edges with a modelling tool for a more rounded edge or use your fingertips, lightly moistened with hand cream.

EMBOSSING AND EMBEDDING

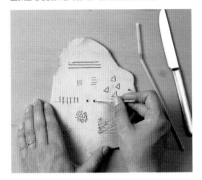

1 Before starting a project that requires surface decoration, practise on a spare piece of clay. Make small holes with a cocktail stick (toothpick), the rounded end of a knife, or by pressing a drinking straw into the clay and removing it with the plug of clay inside. Scratch the surface of the clay and emboss with found objects.

2 Press pieces of broken ceramic into the clay for mosaic work. Ease the surrounding clay gently around the sharp edge of the mosaic pieces to secure them.

3 Designs can be marked out on to the rolled clay by pricking with a needle or hatpin. Use tracing paper for the template, place it over the clay and prick out the design. Remove the template to reveal the design and work over the pinpricks with a knife.

USING READY-MADE MOULDS

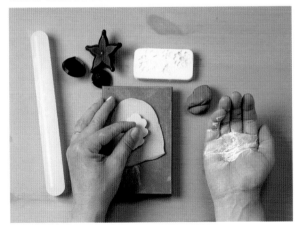

1 Give the mould a very light dusting of talcum powder to prevent it sticking to the clay.

2 Any excess talc can be removed with a water spray or a paintbrush dipped in water: don't make the clay too wet. Always clean the mould to remove particles of clay and dry thoroughly. Brush out any remaining pieces of clay with a bristle paintbrush.

WORKING OVER AN ARMATURE

1 Very large pieces are made over a chicken wire armature. This will reduce the weight of the work. Allow the clay to dry slowly to prevent cracking on both the outside and inside of the armature. Make the armature from chicken wire, cutting and folding with pliers to mould into shape. Protect your hands with gloves.

2 Tear newspaper into strips and paint with diluted PVA (white) glue or wallpaper paste. Drape the strips over the armature to make a thin layer of papier-mâché. This stops the clay from protruding through the holes in the chicken wire as you mould the form.

3 Now start to build the shape with clay. Break off small pieces of clay and flatten them in your hands. Press the clay gently over the frame, smoothing the joins (seams) as you go and pressing the clay into shape.

FILING ROUGH EDGES

When the work is dry, remove rough edges with a nail file or emery board. Sand carefully, as dry clay can be powdery and is delicate. Use a nail file for reaching small areas and fine sandpaper for large surfaces. Seal with PVA glue.

DRYING CLAY

Dry clay slowly to avoid cracking. Cover with a damp cloth or plastic wrap to slow the drying process – especially work that has been made over an armature. Tape small, flat pieces to a firm background to prevent shapes curling, using a weight if necessary. Dry motifs for curved designs over a curved surface. Remove the tape carefully when the work is dry.

REPAIRS

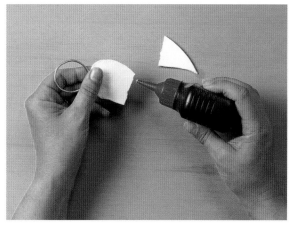

1 Cracks that form while the clay is drying can be
repaired by adding a small amount of water to
clay to form a thick paste. Press the paste into the
crack and allow to dry. Repeat as necessary, then
protect with a coat of PVA (white) glue.

2 Glue broken pieces together with strong wood
glue, then protect with a coat of PVA glue.

DECORATING

1 A variety of decorative
techniques such as sponging
and gilding can be used on
modelling clay. Some types of
self-hardening clay have a tenden-
cy to flake, so it is a good idea to
seal the surface with one or two
coats of PVA (white) glue first.

2 Apply paint with a paintbrush
or sponge, dabbing the bristles
into awkward areas. When the
paint is dry, spray or paint with
varnish to protect the work.
Apply a minimum of two coats,
but check the varnish on a small
area first, as sometimes the colour
alters slightly.

3 If you wish to add surface
decoration, dampen the clay
with water to help the decoration
stick. When dry, check if any clay
is loose and needs repairing. Apply
matt varnish, to seal the surface
and ensure that the relief work
sticks to the base.

TEMPLATES

To enlarge the templates to the desired size, use a photocopier, or trace the design and draw a grid of evenly spaced squares over your tracing. Draw a larger grid on another piece of paper and copy the outline square by square. Draw over the lines to make sure they are continuous.

SILVER-LEAF FINIALS, PP 34–7

VERDIGRIS CLOCK, PP 78–81

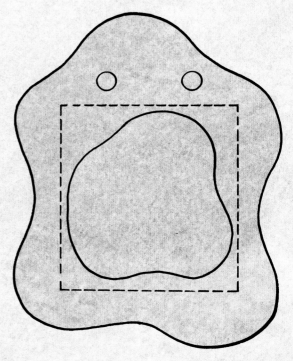

DECORATED FLOWERPOTS, PP 11–15

MOSAIC MIRROR, PP 48–51

BACCHUS GARDEN PLAQUE, PP 30–3

FLORENTINE BOXES, PP 60–3

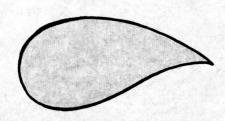

FLORAL LINEN SCENTERS, PP 45–7

FLEUR-DE-LYS WASTEBASKET, PP 74–7

LEAF WALL PLAQUES, PP 42–4

HEN MESSAGE BOARD, PP 24–6

ROCOCO WALL PLAQUE, PP 56–9

FLOWER GARDEN CHALK BOARD, PP 8–10

SUPPLIERS

The specialist materials and equipment that you will require for the modelling clay projects featured in this book are available from any good art supply or cake decorating shop.

Craft World
Head Office
8 North Street
Guildford
Surrey GU1 4AF
Craft superstores nationwide. All craft supplies including special paint effect kits, modelling clay, tools and equipment.

London Sugarart Centre
12 Selkirk Road
London SW17 0ES
Moulds and cutters for making flowers. Small rolling pins and mats. Will do mail order.

Alec Tiranti Ltd
70 High Street
Theale
Reading
Berkshire RG7 5AR
Modelling clay, modelling tools, gold and silver leaf.

Pearl Cake Decorating
22nd Street
New York, NY 10001
USA

Dock Blick
PO Box 1267
Galesburg, IL 61402
USA

ACKNOWLEDGEMENTS

The publishers would like to thank the following people for designing the projects in this book: Penny Boylan for the Decorated Flowerpots pp 11–15, Rose Drawer Handles pp 16–19, Gilded Curtain Tie-backs pp 20–3, Hen Message Board pp 24–6, Geometric Picture Frames pp 38–41, Leaf Wall Plaques pp 42–4, Floral Linen Scenters pp 45–7, Coil Pot pp 67–9 and Stone-effect Platters pp 70–3; Alison Jenkins for the Textured Lamp Base pp 52–5, Flower Garden Chalk Board pp 8–10, Summer Vase pp 27–9 and Silver-leaf Finials pp 34–7; Lucinda Ganderton for the Bacchus Garden Plaque pp 30–3, Mexican Candlesticks pp 64–6; Florentine Boxes pp 60–3; Fleur-de-lys Wastebasket pp 74–7 and Verdigris Clock pp 78–81; Cheryl Owen for the Mosaic Mirror pp 48–51 and Rococo Wall Plaque pp 56–9.

INDEX